Into the Blue Reach

Black Lawrence Press
www.blacklawrence.com

Executive Editor: Diane Goettel
Book Design: Steven Seighman

Black Lawrence Press
115 Center Ave
Aspinwall, PA 15215
U.S.A.

Published 2010 by Black Lawrence Press, an imprint of Dzanc Books

Cover image: *Deep in July*, by John Moran

ISBN: 978-0-9826228-4-1

First edition 2010

Printed in the United States

Into the Blue Reach

*Selected Poems and Prose by
Rainer Maria Rilke*

Translated by

Ingrid Amalia Herbert
and
Alison Kolodinsky

Black Lawrence Press
New York

Inhalt

I

II

Contents

A special note of gratitude to
Uta Rollins and Karen Samuels
for never breaking faith with us.

This book is dedicated with love
to our husbands, Andreas and Rick.

INTRODUCTION

Shortly after 9/11, I flew to Germany for the first time. My friend, Uta Rollins, and I were traveling to Bavaria to visit her family. I nearly decided against going because only two weeks had passed since that infamous day, but at the last minute I decided to keep my ticket. Little did I know that, had I stayed behind, this book would never have been born.

While we were there, we attended a birthday party given in honor of Uta's brother. Since I had nothing on hand to offer as a gift, I gave him what I'd brought along to read on the trip: Stephen Mitchell's well-known *Ahead of All Parting: The Selected Poetry and Prose of Rainer Maria Rilke*. He was genuinely thrilled with this gift.

Before we left Germany, Uta's brother gave me, as a kind of gift in return, the first CD of the Rilke Projekt, entitled "Bis an alle Sterne/To all the stars." The award-winning Rilke Projekt consists of three audio CDs, the first of which had been released nine months earlier in January, 2001. On each track, Rilke's poems or prose pieces are performed by actors and/or vocalists with the accompaniment of an orchestra.

The masterminds behind the Rilke Projekt are Richard Schönherz and Angelica Fleer who went on to compose the two sequels, "In meinem wilden Herzen/In my wild heart," and "Überfließende Himmel/Overflowing heavens," released in 2002 and 2004 respectively. A DVD was released as well in April of 2005, made from tapes of the hugely successful international tour and starring many of the original cast.

Receiving that CD was the beginning of *Into the Blue Reach*. When I returned home in October 2001, I began to research the texts performed on each of the tracks of "Bis an alle Sterne." I was so taken by the riveting performances, the wonderful music, and the beautiful German language that I began to buy volumes of poetry by various English translators of Rilke, hoping to discover what the words performed on each track meant. (All of the liner notes, unfortunately for me, were in German.) My bookshelves, now heavy with volumes of Rilke, are home to the works of many notable translators including Stephen Mitchell, Edward Snow, John J. L. Mood, C. F. MacIntyre, Joanna Macy, M. D. Herbert Norton, Robert Bly, Galway Kinnel, Bernard Frank, J. B. Leischman, and Walter Arndt. Although these volumes offered me some wonderful reading, many of the poems performed on "Bis an alle Sterne" remained a mystery.

In 2003, Uta's sister, Ingrid Herbert, came to Florida for a visit. I had met Ingrid previously, but it was at this time that Uta suggested Ingrid and I work together. Ingrid is bilingual and has a keen interest in Rilke and poetry, though she is not a poet herself. From the very first moment I mentioned what I was after—to decipher all the tracks on "Bis an alle Sterne"—Ingrid was game.

And so our collaboration began—the two of us emailing one another across the Atlantic. Although emailing notes back and forth was time-consuming and sometimes frustrating, the beauty of that particular method was that all our ideas were in print. We'd email the most general and the minutest of details and ideas to each other; not just definitions and conjectures, but also prosody, scansion, etc., which I taught her as we went along.

Things moved more quickly when we could work together, day after day, for a few weeks at a time, in person. This we did on four occasions over three and a half years. Ingrid flew to Florida or to Bowen Island where my husband and I have a summer home. When we worked at my house, we worried about nothing but Rilke until my husband rang the dinner bell. Two translators have never been more spoiled. During the spring of 2005, I was able to spend more than two weeks at her home in Germany.

By the early winter of 2006, we finished the book: twenty-five poems and prose pieces in all, containing translations for every track on "Bis an alle Sterne." We also included other translations: three poems ("Engellieder/Angel Songs," "Ernste Stunde/Grave Hour," and "Vorgefühl/Presentiment") from the second CD, as well as two poems from the third CD—("Herbsttag/Autumn Day") and an untitled poem "[Vor lauter Lauschen und Staunen]/ [For the sake of listening and wondering]." *Into the Blue Reach* also includes three of Rilke's poems which are not part of the Rilke Projekt: ("Abend/Evening"), ("Der Dichter/The Poet"), and ("Schlußstück/End Point").

Many have asked us how we worked together: I didn't speak, read or write German and Ingrid is not a poet. Surprisingly, it worked out perfectly. We discovered early on that Ingrid was most comfortable translating without any aids, other than her dictionary and thesaurus. Here is how we'd begin: Ingrid would write out her translation without consulting any other translator's work. Then we would go over it together, scan each line, discuss the meaning and intention of Rilke's work, and talk about the overall text in its relationship to the period in which Rilke wrote it. Only when we had completed our own translation or were especially curious about a specific line did we consult the work of another translator, if a translation could be found.

Neither Ingrid nor I mean to minimize the tremendous contribution people such as Edward Snow and Stephen Mitchell have made. Were it not for both of these men in particular, Rilke would not be as well-read as he is in the United States.

But now on the scene are translators who work in much the same way as Ingrid and I do. The Russian-born translator, Larissa Volokhonsky, and her American-born husband, Richard Pevear, collaborate to produce works which have garnered considerable acclaim. Their most recent release of Leo Tolstoy's *War and Peace* follows many novels by Dostoevsky, Chekhov, and Gogol. Volokhonsky and Pevear describe their two-step process in the following way: she hammers out a literal translation of the work, and he adapts her translation into stylistically meaningful English. Then they begin reviewing the drafts together until each is satisfied.

In other aspects of the work, Ingrid and I have broken with some of the practices of our peers. Where American and Canadian translators often choose to keep end rhymes, for example, we decided to break that rule. It was a choice that we made early on. Instead, we use internal rhyme so as to maintain the integrity of both sound and meaning as much as possible. We paid particular attention to keeping the number of feet per line. Although this was not always feasible, we worked painstakingly to do so whenever possible.

Nor did we interject words that were not Rilke's own. To do so is enticing, but because we were a team it was easier to help each other avoid that trap. This was probably the singular issue that bothered us the most: that many translators substituted or padded translations with words which were not in Rilke's work, whether it be for the sake of an end rhyme or illuminating a passage. To remain faithful to the original language was always at the forefront of our work. In just this way, we will continue to translate Rilke's poems and prose.

Alison Kolodinsky
Bowen Island, BC
July 18, 2008

— I —

[Vergiß, vergiß]

Vergiß, vergiß, und laß uns jetzt nur dies
erleben, wie die Sterne durch geklärten
Nachthimmel dringen, wie der Mond die Gärten
voll übersteigt. Wir fühlten längst schon, wies
spiegelnder wird im Dunkeln; wie ein Schein
entsteht, ein weißer Schatten in dem Glanz
der Dunkelheit. Nun aber laß uns ganz
hinübertreten in die Welt hinein
die monden ist—

- Paris, Sommer 1909

[Forget, forget]

Forget, forget, and let us now live
to see only this, how the stars pervade
the bared night sky, how the cirque of the moon
fully scales the gardens. For so long
we've sensed how reflection deepens in the dark;
how a gleam emerges, a white shadow
in the sheen of darkness. But now
let us completely step into the world
which is moon—

- Paris, summer 1909

Zum Einschlafen zu sagen

Ich möchte jemanden einsingen,
bei jemandem sitzen und sein.
Ich möchte dich wiegen und kleinsingen
und begleiten schlafaus und schlafein.
Ich möchte der Einzige sein im Haus,
der wüßte: die Nacht war kalt.
Und ich möchte horchen herein und hinaus
in dich, in die Welt, in den Wald.
Die Uhren rufen sich schlagend an,
und man sieht der Zeit auf den Grund.
Und unten geht noch ein fremder Mann
und stört einen fremden Hund.
Dahinter wird Stille. Ich habe groß
die Augen auf dich gelegt;
und sie halten dich sanft und lassen dich los,
wenn ein Ding sich im Dunkel bewegt.

To Say for Going to Sleep

I would like to sing someone to sleep,
to sit beside someone and be.
I would like to rock you and calm you by singing
and go with you from and to sleep.
I would like to be the only one in the house
who knew: the night was cold.
And I'd like to listen inward and out
into you, the world, the woods.
The clocks call to each other by striking,
and one sees to the bottom of time.
And yet, below, a strange man walks
and rouses a strange dog.
After that comes stillness.
I have laid my eyes upon you wide;
and they hold you softly and let you go,
when some thing moves in the dark.

Lied

Du, der ichs nicht sage, daß ich bei Nacht
weinend liege,
deren Wesen mich müde macht
wie eine Wiege.
Du, die mir nicht sagt, wenn sie wacht
meinetwillen:
wie, wenn wir diese Pracht
ohne zu stillen
in uns ertrügen?

  –   –   –

Sieh dir die Liebenden an,
wenn erst das Bekennen begann,
wie bald sie lügen.

  –   –   –

Du machst mich allein. Dich einzig kann ich vertauschen.
Eine Weile bist dus, dann wieder ist es das Rauschen,
oder es ist ein Duft ohne Rest.
Ach, in den Armen hab ich sie alle verloren,
du nur, du wirst immer wieder geboren:
weil ich niemals dich anhielt, halt ich dich fest.

Song

You, whom I do not tell, that by night
I lie weeping,
whose tranquil nature quiets me
like a cradle.
When, for me, you stay awake
you do not tell:
how would it be if
we inwardly endured this splendor,
without it being eased?

   -    -   -

Look at the lovers,
once the confession has begun,
how soon they lie.

   -    -   -

You make me alone. I confound only
you with other things. Sometimes it is you,
at times it is the murmur, or a scent without a trace.
Ah, from my arms I have lost them all,
you only, you are born again and again:
because I never hindered you, I hold you fast.

Liebes-Lied

Wie soll ich meine Seele halten, daß
sie nicht an deine rührt? Wie soll ich sie
hinheben über dich zu andern Dingen?
Ach gerne möcht ich sie bei irgendwas
Verlorenem im Dunkel unterbringen
an einer fremden stillen Stelle, die
nicht weiterschwingt, wenn deine Tiefen schwingen.
Doch alles, was uns anrührt, dich und mich,
nimmt uns zusammen wie ein Bogenstrich,
der aus zwei Saiten *eine* Stimme zieht.
Auf welches Instrument sind wir gespannt?
Und welcher Geiger hat uns in der Hand?
O süßes Lied.

Love Song

How shall I hold back my soul, so that
it does not touch yours? How shall I
lift it over you toward other things?
Ah I would like to hold it safe
with what is lost in the darkness
at an unknown silent place, which
does not keep swaying when your depths stir.
Yet everything that touches us, you and me,
brings us together like the stroke of a bow
that draws *one* voice from two strings.
On what instrument are we made taut?
And what fiddler has us in his hand?
Oh sweet song.

[Welche Wiesen duften deine Hände]

Welche Wiesen duften deine Hände?
Fühlst du wie auf deine Widerstände
stärker sich der Duft von draußen stützt.
Drüber stehn die Sterne schon in Bildern.
Gib mir, Liebe, deinen Mund zu mildern;
ach, dein ganzes Haar ist unbenützt.

Sieh, ich will dich mit dir selbst umgeben
und die welkende Erwartung heben
von dem Rande deiner Augenbraun;
wie mit lauter Liderinnenseiten
will ich dir mit meinen Zärtlichkeiten
alle Stellen schließen, welche schaun.

[Which meadows scent your hands]

Which meadows scent your hands?
Do you feel how the fragrance is sustained
all the more by your resistance.
Already the stars pose in images above.
Give me, love, your mouth to soothe;
ah, your untouched hair.

See, I wish to encompass you with you
and lift the fading anticipation
from the edges of your brows;
for you, with all my tenderness
solely like the eyelids' inner pages
I want to close all places which look.

Die Liebende

Ja ich sehne mich nach dir. Ich gleite
mich verlierend selbst mir aus der Hand,
ohne Hoffnung, daß ich das bestreite,
was zu mir kommt wie aus deiner Seite
ernst und unbeirrt und unverwandt.

...jene Zeiten: O wie war ich Eines,
nichts was rief und nichts was mich verriet;
meine Stille war wie eines Steines,
über den der Bach sein Murmeln zieht.

Aber jetzt in diesen Frühlingswochen
hat mich etwas langsam abgebrochen
von dem unbewußten dunkeln Jahr.
Etwas hat mein armes warmes Leben
irgendeinem in die Hand gegeben,
der nicht weiß was ich noch gestern war.

Woman in Love

Yes, I long for you. I slip,
losing myself from my own grasp
without hope of disputing this,
that what comes to me is from your core,
serious and steadfast and undeterred.

...those times: Oh, how I was one with myself,
nothing called and nothing revealed me;
my tranquility was like a stone's,
over which the rivulet pulls its murmur.

But now in these weeks of spring
something has slowly severed me
from the dark, insentient year.
Something has placed my poor warm life
into the hand of some anyone
who's unaware of what I was only yesterday.

[Nenn ich dich Aufgang oder Untergang]

Nenn ich dich Aufgang oder Untergang?
Denn manchmal bin ich vor dem Morgen bang
und greife scheu nach seiner Rosen Röte—
und ahne eine Angst in seiner Flöte
vor Tagen, welche liedlos sind und lang.

Aber die Abende sind mild und mein,
von meinem Schauen sind sie still beschienen;
in meinen Armen schlafen Wälder ein—
und ich bin selbst das Klingen über ihnen,
und mit dem Dunkel in den Violinen
verwandt durch all mein Dunkelsein.

[Do I name you rising or falling]

Do I name you rising or falling?
Because sometimes I am wary of daybreak
and shyly reach for its roses' redness—
and sense anxiety in its flute
of days, empty of music and long.

But the evenings are mild and mine,
quietly shone upon by my gaze,
forests fall to sleep in my arms—
and I'm even the clinking above them,
and in tune with the dark space inside violins,
for the sake of all my darkness.

[Irgendwo blüht die Blume des Abschieds]

Irgendwo blüht die Blume des Abschieds und streut
immerfort Blütenstaub, den wir atmen, herüber;
auch noch im kommendsten Wind atmen wir
Abschied.

[Somewhere the flower of parting blooms]

Somewhere the flower of parting blooms and scatters
its pollen endlessly to here, which we inhale;
even in the utmost coming wind, we breathe
farewell.

Der Tod der Geliebten

Er wußte nur vom Tod was alle wissen:
daß er uns nimmt und in das Stumme stößt.
Als aber sie, nicht von ihm fortgerissen,
nein, leis aus seinen Augen ausgelöst,

hinüberglitt zu unbekannten Schatten,
und als er fühlte, daß sie drüben nun
wie einen Mond ihr Mädchenlächeln hatten
und ihre Weise wohlzutun:

da wurden ihm die Toten so bekannt,
als wäre er durch sie mit einem jeden
ganz nah verwandt; er ließ die andern reden

und glaubte nicht und nannte jenes Land
das gutgelegene, das immersüße—
Und tastete es ab für ihre Füße.

The Death of the Beloved

He only knew of death what's known to all:
it takes us and hurls us into muteness.
Yet when she, not ripped away from him,
no, quietly undone from his eyes,

drifted over to unknown shadows,
and when he sensed that on the other side,
they had her young girl's smile like a moon
and her goodness:

then the dead grew so familiar to him,
as if he were, through her, closely related
to every one; he let the others talk

and disbelieved and named that land
the well-lodged place, the eversweet—
And touched upon it for her feet.

[Wie das Gestirn, der Mond]

Wie das Gestirn, der Mond, erhaben, voll Anlaß,
plötzlich die Höhn übertritt, die entworfene Nacht
gelassen vollendend: siehe: so steigt mir
rein die Stimme hervor aus Gebirgen des Nichtmehr.

Und die Stellen, erstaunt, an denen du dawarst und
fortkamst, schmerzen klarer dir nach.

- Paris, Herbst 1913

[As the heavenly body, the moon]

As the heavenly body, the moon, sublime, resolute,
abruptly steps over the heights, calmly completing
the outlined night: look: so my voice rises,
pure, out of the mountains which cease to exist.
And the places, bewildered, from which you came away,
ache more clearly for you.

- Paris, autumn 1913

— II —

[Jetzt wär es Zeit]

Jetzt wär es Zeit, daß Götter träten aus
bewohnten Dingen...
Und daß sie jede Wand in meinem Haus
umschlügen. Neue Seite. Nur der Wind,
den solches Blatt im Wenden würfe, reichte hin,
die Luft, wie eine Scholle, umzuschaufeln:
ein neues Atemfeld. Oh Götter, Götter!
Ihr Oftgekommenen, Schläfer in den Dingen,
die heiter aufstehn, die sich an den Brunnen,
die wir vermuten, Hals und Antlitz waschen
und die ihr Ausgeruhtsein leicht hinzutun
zu dem, was voll scheint, unserm vollen Leben.
Noch einmal sei es euer Morgen, Götter.
Wir wiederholen. Ihr allein seid Ursprung.
Die Welt steht auf mit euch, und Anfang glänzt
an allen Bruchstellen unseres Mißlingens...

- Muzot, Oktober 1925

[Now would be the time]

Now would be the time that gods stepped out
of inhabited things...
And that they would bring down every wall
in my house. New page. Only the wind,
summoned by turning such a page, would suffice
to upend the air as a shovel tosses earth:
a new breathfield. Oh gods, gods!
You who came so often, sleepers in things,
who rise serenely, who wash neck and face
at wellsprings we can only imagine,
and who, with ease, add your restedness
to what seems filled, our full life.
Once again it shall be your morning, gods.
We say once more. You alone are the source.
The world gets up with you, and beginning shines
on all the cracks of our failure...

- Muzot, October 1925

Vorgefühl

Ich bin wie eine Fahne von Fernen umgeben.
Ich ahne die Winde, die kommen, und muß
    sie leben,
während die Dinge unten sich noch nicht rühren:
die Türen schließen noch sanft, und in den
    Kaminen ist Stille;
die Fenster zittern noch nicht, und der Staub ist
    noch schwer.

Da weiß ich die Stürme schon und bin erregt wie
    das Meer.
Und breite mich aus und falle in mich hinein
und werfe mich ab und bin ganz allein
in dem großen Sturm.

Presentiment

I am like a flag surrounded by open space.
 I sense the winds, which will come, and must live
    through them,
while all things below do not yet move:
the doors still close softly, and silence fills
    the chimneys;
 the windows do not rattle yet, and the dust is
    still at rest.

Even now I know these storms and am in turmoil
    like the sea.
I unfold myself and then fall back into myself
and shed myself and am utterly alone
in the great storm.

[Du mußt das Leben nicht verstehen]

Du mußt das Leben nicht verstehen,
dann wird es werden wie ein Fest.
Und laß dir jeden Tag geschehen
so wie ein Kind im Weitergehen
von jedem Wehen
sich viele Blüten schenken läßt.

Sie aufzusammeln und zu sparen,
das kommt dem Kind nicht in den Sinn.
Es löst sie leise aus den Haaren,
drin sie so gern gefangen waren,
und hält den lieben jungen Jahren
nach neuen seine Hände hin.

[You do not need to understand life]

You do not need to understand life,
and then it will be like a festival.
And let every day happen to you
the way a child, going along
receives many blossoms
as a gift from each breeze.

To gather them up and save them
does not enter the child's mind.
She releases them gently from her hair,
where they were happily held captive,
and to the lovely young years
she holds out her hands for more.

Der Panther

Im Jardin des Plantes, Paris

Sein Blick ist vom Vorübergehn der Stäbe
so müd geworden, daß er nichts mehr hält.
Ihm ist, als ob es tausend Stäbe gäbe
und hinter tausend Stäben keine Welt.

Der weiche Gang geschmeidig starker Schritte,
der sich im allerkleinsten Kreise dreht,
ist wie ein Tanz von Kraft um eine Mitte,
in der betäubt ein großer Wille steht.

Nur manchmal schiebt der Vorhang der Pupille
sich lautlos auf—. Dann geht ein Bild hinein,
geht durch der Glieder angespannte Stille—
und hört im Herzen auf zu sein.

The Panther

In the Jardin des Plantes, Paris

His gaze, from the passing of the bars
has grown so weary, it holds nothing more.
He feels as if there were a thousand bars
and beyond the thousand bars, no world.

The muted pace of strong, fluid strides,
which turns around the smallest possible circle,
is like a dance of strength around some center
in which a powerful will stands numbed.

Only sometimes, soundlessly, the pupil's shutter
pushes itself open—. Then an image enters,
circuits the tense stillness of the limbs—
and in the heart stops being.

[Ich fürchte mich so vor der Menschen Wort]

Ich fürchte mich so vor der Menschen Wort.
Sie sprechen alles so deutlich aus:
Und dieses heißt Hund und jenes heißt Haus,
und hier ist Beginn und das Ende ist dort.

Mich bangt auch ihr Sinn, ihr Spiel mit dem Spott.
Sie wissen alles, was wird und war;
kein Berg ist ihnen mehr wunderbar;
ihr Garten und Gut grenzt grade an Gott.

Ich will immer warnen und wehren: Bleibt fern.
Die Dinge singen hör ich so gern.
Ihr rührt sie an: sie sind starr und stumm.
Ihr bringt mir alle die Dinge um.

[I so fear the word of mankind]

I so fear the word of mankind.
They pronounce everything so precisely:
And this means dog and that means house,
and here's the beginning and the end is there.

I don't trust their spirit, their sport of mockery,
they know all, what will be and was;
no mountain is magic to them anymore;
their land and belongings border on God.

I constantly want to ward off: Keep away.
To hear the song in things gives me joy.
You touch them: they become silent and still.
In my world you kill every thing.

Menschen bei Nacht

Die Nächte sind nicht für die Menge gemacht.
Von deinem Nachbar trennt dich die Nacht,
und du sollst ihn nicht suchen trotzdem.
Und machst du nachts deine Stube licht,
um Menschen zu schauen ins Angesicht,
so mußt du bedenken: wem.

Die Menschen sind furchtbar vom Licht entstellt,
das von ihren Gesichtern träuft,
und haben sie nachts sich zusammengesellt,
so schaust du eine wankende Welt
durcheinandergehäuft.
Auf ihren Stirnen hat gelber Schein
alle Gedanken verdrängt,
in ihren Blicken flackert der Wein,
an ihren Händen hängt
die schwere Gebärde, mit der sie sich
bei ihren Gesprächen verstehn;
und dabei sagen sie: *Ich* und *Ich*
und meinen: Irgendwen.

Human Beings by Night

The nights are not made for the masses.
Night divides you from your neighbor,
and even so you're not to seek him out.
And when you light your little room at night,
to look someone in the face,
then you must consider: whom.

Humans are dreadfully disfigured by the light,
which drips from their faces,
and should they gather at night,
then you'll see a wavery world
all heaped up together.
On their foreheads a jaundiced shine
has driven out all thoughts,
the wine flickers in their glances,
the heavy gesture hangs on their hands
by which they comprehend
one another in conversations;
and by it they say: *I* and *I*
and mean: Anyone.

Der Dichter

Du entfernst dich von mir, du Stunde.
Wunden schlägt mir dein Flügelschlag.
Allein: was soll ich mit meinem Munde?
mit meiner Nacht? mit meinem Tag?

Ich habe keine Geliebte, kein Haus,
keine Stelle auf der ich lebe.
Alle Dinge, an die ich mich gebe,
werden reich und geben mich aus.

The Poet

You, hour, you take your leave of me.
I am wounded by your wing's beating.
Alone: what shall I do with my mouth?
with my night? with my day?

I have no beloved, no house,
no plot of land on which I live.
All things, to which I give myself,
are enriched and exhaust me.

Engellieder

ICH ließ meinen Engel lange nicht los,
und er verarmte mir in den Armen
und wurde klein, und ich wurde groß
und auf einmal war ich das Erbarmen,
und er eine zitternde Bitte bloß.

Da hab ich ihm seine Himmel gegeben,—
und er ließ mir das Nahe, daraus er entschwand;
er lernte das Schweben, ich lernte das Leben,
und wir haben langsam einander erkannt...

SEIT mich mein Engel nicht mehr bewacht,
kann er frei seine Flügel entfalten
und die Stille der Sterne durchspalten,—
denn er muß meiner einsamen Nacht
nicht mehr die ängstlichen Hände halten—
seit mich mein Engel nicht mehr bewacht.

Angel Songs

FOR a long time I would not let my angel go,
and he became poor in my arms
and he became small, and I became large
and suddenly I was mercy,
and he, only a trembling supplicant.

Therefore I gave him his heavens,—
he left me all that was within reach, and vanished;
he learned to float, I learned life,
and slowly we understood one another...

SINCE my angel does not guard me anymore,
he can spread his wings unencumbered
and cleave the stars' silence,—
for he must no longer hold
the frightened hands of my lonely night—
since my angel does not guard me anymore.

HAT auch mein Engel keine Pflicht mehr,
seit ihn mein strenger Tag vertrieb,
oft senkt er sehnend sein Gesicht her
und hat die Himmel nicht mehr lieb.

Er möchte wieder aus armen Tagen
über der Wälder rauschendem Ragen
meine blassen Gebete tragen
in die Heimat der Cherubim.

Dorthin trug er mein frühes Weinen
und Bedanken, und meine kleinen
Leiden wuchsen dorten zu Hainen,
welche flüstern über ihm...

WENN ich einmal im Lebensland,
im Gelärme von Markt und Messe—
meiner Kindheit erblühte Blässe:
meinen ernsten Engel vergesse—
seine Güte und sein Gewand,
die betenden Hände, die segnende Hand,—
in meinen heimlichsten Träumen behalten
werde ich immer das Flügelfalten,
das wie eine weiße Zypresse
hinter ihm stand...

THOUGH my angel has no duties anymore,
ever since my immutable day drove him away,
he often lowers his face wistfully
and no longer loves the heavens.

Again he would like to carry
my colorless prayers from the poor days
over the tops of rustling trees
to the home of the cherubim.

He carried to that dwelling place
my past tears and gratitude, and there
my small sufferings grew into groves
whispering over him...

IF I should ever, in the land of the living,
in the clamor of market and fair,
in the ripened paleness of my childhood,
forget my solemn angel—
his goodness and his robe,
the praying hands, the blessing hand,—
in my most secret dreams
I will always remember the folding of wings,
that stood behind him
like a white cypress...

SEINE Hände blieben wie blinde
Vögel, die, um Sonne betrogen,
wenn die andern über die Wogen
zu den währenden Lenzen zogen,
in der leeren, entlaubten Linde
wehren müssen dem Winterwinde.

Auf seinen Wangen war die Scham
der Bräute, die über der Seele Schrecken
dunkle Purpurdecken
breiten dem Bräutigam.

Und in den Augen lag
Glanz von dem ersten Tag,—
aber weit über allem war
ragend das tragende Flügelpaar...

UM die vielen Madonnen sind
viele ewige Engelknaben,
die Verheißung und Heimat haben
in dem Garten, wo Gott beginnt.

HIS hands remained like blind birds,
which, cheated of sunlight
when the others migrated over the waves
to everlasting springtimes,
must fend off the winter wind
in the bare, defoliated linden tree.

On his cheeks was the shame
of brides who, for the groom, unfold
dark purple covers
over the soul's fright.

And in the eyes
was brightness from the first day,—
but towering high over everything
was the herculean pair of wings...

SURROUNDING the many Madonnas
are many eternal angel boys,
whose Promised Land is their home
in the garden, where God begins.

Und sie ragen alle nach Rang,
und sie tragen die goldenen Geigen,
und die Schönsten dürfen nie schweigen:
ihre Seelen sind aus Gesang.
Immer wieder müssen sie
klingen alle die dunkeln Chorale,
die sie klangen vieltausend Male:
Gott stieg nieder aus seinem Strahle
und du warst die schönste Schale
Seiner Sehnsucht, Madonna Marie.

Aber oft in der Dämmerung
wird die Mutter müder und müder,—
und dann flüstern die Engelbrüder,
und sie jubeln sie wieder jung.
Und sie winken mit den weißen
Flügeln festlich im Hallenhofe,
und sie heben aus den heißen
Herzen höher die eine Strophe:
Alle, die in Schönheit gehn,
werden in Schönheit auferstehn.

And they all reach for position,
and they carry the golden violins,
and the most beautiful can never be silent:
their souls are made of hymns.
Again and again they must
ring all the dark chorales,
which they have rung thousands of times:
God stepped down, out of His beam of sun
and you were the most beautiful shell
of His longing, Madonna Maria.

But often at twilight
the Holy Mother grows tired, more and more,—
and then the angel brothers whisper,
and they cheer for her to feel young again.
And they wave splendidly
in the hallowed hall with their white wings,
and from burning hearts
they lift higher this one verse:
All who depart in beauty,
will rise in beauty.

Abend

Einsam hinterm letzten Haus
geht die rote Sonne schlafen,
und in ernste Schlußoktaven
klingt des Tages Jubel aus.

Lose Lichter haschen spät
noch sich auf den Dächerkanten,
wenn die Nacht schon Diamanten
in die blauen Fernen sät.

Evening

Lonesome behind the last house
the red sun goes to sleep,
and the day's jubilation fades
into solemn, final octaves.

Late beams of unfettered light
still angle for rooflines,
even as night sows diamonds
into the blue reach.

Für Hans Carossa

Auch noch Verlieren ist *unser*; und selbst das Vergessen
hat noch Gestalt in dem bleibenden Reich der Verwandlung.
Losgelassenes kreist; und sind wir auch selten die Mitte
einem der Kreise: sie ziehn um uns die heile Figur.

For Hans Carossa

Yet losing is *ours* as well; and even oblivion
still has form in the immutable realm of change.
What we let go circles; and though we seldom are the center
of circles: they draw around us the unbroken figure.

Herbsttag

Herr: es ist Zeit. Der Sommer war sehr groß.
Leg deinen Schatten auf die Sonnenuhren,
und auf den Fluren laß die Winde los.

Befiehl den letzten Früchten voll zu sein;
Gieb ihnen noch zwei südlichere Tage,
dränge sie zur Vollendung hin und jage
die letzte Süße in den schweren Wein.

Wer jetzt kein Haus hat, baut sich keines mehr.
Wer jetzt allein ist, wird es lange bleiben,
wird wachen, lesen, lange Briefe schreiben
und wird in den Alleen hin und her
unruhig wandern, wenn die Blätter treiben.

Autumn Day

Lord: it is time. The summer was immense.
Lay your shadow upon the sundials,
and let loose the winds on open fields.

Command the last fruits to fully ripen;
render them two more southerly days,
drive them to a ready perfection and chase
the last sweetness into the heavy wine.

He, who still has no house, will never build one.
He, who is still alone, will remain so a long time,
will stay awake, read, write long letters
and wander restlessly, up and down
the treelined avenues when leaves fly.

Ernste Stunde

Wer jetzt weint irgendwo in der Welt,
    ohne Grund weint in der Welt,
    weint über mich.

Wer jetzt lacht irgendwo in der Nacht,
    ohne Grund lacht in der Nacht,
    lacht mich aus.

Wer jetzt geht irgendwo in der Welt,
    ohne Grund geht in der Welt,
    geht zu mir.

Wer jetzt stirbt irgendwo in der Welt,
    ohne Grund stirbt in der Welt:
    sieht mich an.

Grave Hour

Whoever weeps now anywhere in the world,
    without cause weeps in the world,
    weeps over me.

Whoever laughs now anywhere in the night,
    without cause laughs in the night,
    laughs at me.

Whoever moves now anywhere in the world,
    without cause moves in the world,
    moves toward me.

Whoever dies now anywhere in the world,
    without cause dies in the world:
    looks at me.

[Ich lebe mein Leben in wachsenden Ringen]

Ich lebe mein Leben in wachsenden Ringen,
die sich über die Dinge ziehn.
Ich werde den letzten vielleicht nicht vollbringen,
aber versuchen will ich ihn.

Ich kreise um Gott, um den uralten Turm,
und ich kreise jahrtausendelang;
und ich weiß noch nicht: bin ich ein Falke, ein Sturm
oder ein großer Gesang.

[I live my life in widening rings]

I live my life in widening rings
that reach across all things.
I may never realize the ultimate one,
but I am resolved to try.

I circle around God, the primordial tower,
and I circle for thousands of years;
and I still don't know: am I a falcon, a storm,
or a divine song.

[Vor lauter Lauschen und Staunen]

Vor lauter Lauschen und Staunen sei still,
du mein tieftiefes Leben;
daß du weißt, was der Wind dir will,
eh noch die Birken beben.

Und wenn dir einmal das Schweigen sprach,
laß deine Sinne besiegen.
Jedem Hauche gieb dich, gieb nach,
er wird dich lieben und wiegen.

Und dann meine Seele sei weit, sei weit,
daß dir das Leben gelinge,
breite dich wie ein Feierkleid
über die sinnenden Dinge.

[For the sake of listening and wondering]

For the sake of listening and wondering, be still,
you, my deep-deep life;
that you may know what the wind means for you,
even before the birches tremble.

And should silence ever speak to you,
let your senses be overwhelmed.
Give yourself to every breath, give in,
it will love you and cradle you.

And then my soul be wide, be wide,
so that your life proves worthy,
spread yourself like a celebration gown
over the sentient things.

Schlußstück

Der Tod ist groß.
Wir sind die Seinen
lachenden Munds.
Wenn wir uns mitten im Leben meinen,
wagt er zu weinen
mitten in uns.

End Point

Death is grand.
We are his
with laughing mouth.
When we think we are in the midst of life,
he dares to weep
in the midst of us.

Notes

1. [Vergiß, vergiß]/[Forget, forget] - written in Paris, summer of 1909 (uncollected)

2. Zum Einschlafen zu sagen/To Say for Going to Sleep - from *Das Buch der Bilder: Des ersten Buches zweiter Teil (The Book of Images: the second part of the first book)* (1902 and 1906)

3. Lied/Song - from *Die Aufzeichnungen des Malte Laurids Brigge (The Notebooks of Malte Laurids Brigge)* (1910)

4. Liebes-Lied/Love Song - from *Neue Gedichte: (New Poems)* (1907)

5. [Welche Wiesen duften deine Hände]/[Which meadows scent your hands] - written in the summer of 1909 (uncollected)

6. Die Liebende/Woman in Love - from *Das Buch der Bilder: Des ersten Buches erster Teil (The Book of Images: the first part of the first book)* (1902 and 1906)

7. [Nenn ich dich Aufgang oder Untergang]/[Do I name you rising or falling] - from *Mir zur Feier (For Me to Celebrate)* (1909)

8. [Irgendwo blüht die Blume des Abschieds]/[Somewhere the flower of parting blooms] - written at Muzot in mid-October, 1924 (uncollected)

9. Der Tod der Geliebten/The Death of the Beloved - from *Neue Gedichte: Der neuen Gedichte anderer Teil (New Poems: the new poems' other part)* (1908)

10. [Wie das Gestirn, der Mond]/[As the heavenly body, the moon] - written in Paris, autumn, 1913 (uncollected)

11. [Jetzt wär es Zeit]/[Now would be the time] - written at Muzot in October, 1925 (uncollected)

12. Vorgefühl/Presentiment - from *Das Buch der Bilder: Des ersten Buches zweiter Teil (The Book of Images: the second part of the first book)* (1902 and 1906)

13. [Du mußt das Leben nicht verstehen]/[You do not need to understand life] - from *Mir zur Feier (For Me to Celebrate)* (1909)

14. Der Panther/The Panther - from *Neue Gedichte (New Poems)* (1907)

15. [Ich fürchte mich so vor der Menschen Wort]/[I so fear the word of mankind] - from *Mir zur Feier (For Me to Celebrate)* (1909)

16. Menschen bei Nacht/Human Beings by Night - from *Das Buch der Bilder: Des ersten Buches zweiter Teil (The Book of Images: the second part of the first book)* (1902 and 1906)

17. Der Dichter/The Poet - from *Neue Gedichte (New Poems)* (1907)

18. Engellieder/Angel Songs - from *Mir zur Feier (For Me to Celebrate)* (1909)

19. Abend/Evening - from *Larenopfer* (1895)

20. Für Hans Carossa/For Hans Carossa - written February 7, 1924 as a dedication in a copy of *Duino Elegies* for his doctor friend, Hans Carossa (uncollected)

21. Herbsttag/Autumn Day - from *Das Buch der Bilder: Des ersten Buches zweiter Teil (The Book of Images: the second part of the first book)* (1902 and 1906)

22. Ernste Stunde/Grave Hour - from *Das Buch der Bilder: Des ersten Buches zweiter Teil (The Book of Images: the second part of the first book)* (1902 and 1906)

23. [Ich lebe mein Leben in wachsenden Ringen]/[I live my life in widening rings] - from *Das Stundenbuch: Das Buch vom mönchischen Leben (The Book of Hours: the Book of Monastic Life)* (1899)

24. [Vor lauter Lauschen und Staunen]/[For the sake of listening and wondering] - from *Mir zur Feier (For Me to Celebrate)* (1909)

25. Schlußstück/End Point - from *Das Buch der Bilder: Des zweiten Buches zweiter Teil (The Book of Images: the second part of the second book)* (1902 and 1906)

About the Author

RAINER MARIA RILKE (4. Dec. 1875 – 29. Dec. 1926) was born
Rene Karl Wilhelm Johann Joseph Maria Rilke in Prague, Bohemia
(now the Czech Republic). He is to this day still regarded as one
of the most distinguished poets of the German language. Rilke
authored verse, highly lyrical prose, a novel, essays, narrations,
and a play, as well as numerous translations of literature and
lyrics from the French and other languages. An important part
of his literary work is his considerable correspondence to friends
including Marina Tsvetaeva, Auguste Rodin, and Boris Pasternak.
He died of leukemia at the age of 51 at the Valmont Sanatorium in
Switzerland—his homeland by choice.

About the Translators

INGRID AMALIA HERBERT was a student of English in Bournemouth, Great Britain. She has worked as a trainer and teacher at the Lufthansa Flight Training Center in Frankfurt. A native of Bavaria, she lives with her husband Andreas in Alzenau, Germany. Her passions include travelling, gardening, winemaking from their own apple orchard, and of course, Rilke.

ALISON KOLODINSKY is a poet and translator, and the recipient of an Individual Artist Fellowship from the Florida Arts Council. Her poems have appeared in many anthologies, magazines and reviews including *Poetry, Alaska Quarterly Review*, and *Cream City Review*. Her first collection of poetry is forthcoming in the fall of 2010 from MotesBooks and is entitled *Inventing the Wind*. Kolodinsky also has a Master of Science Degree in Community/Clinical Psychology. She and Rick, her husband of 30 years, divide their time between New Smyrna Beach, Florida and Bowen Island, British Columbia.